Reaching Out to Mothers: Public Health and Child Welfare

European Association for the History of Medicine and Health Publications

Editors on behalf of the European Association for the History of Medicine and Health
Robert Jütte and John Woodward

Academic inquiries regarding the publications should be addressed to:

John Woodward, Sheffield Centre for the History of Medicine,
University of Sheffield, Sheffield S10 2TN, United Kingdom

or

Robert Jütte, Institut für Geschichte der Medizin der Robert Bosch Stiftung,
Straussweg 17, D-70184 Stuttgart, Germany

All sales inquiries should be addressed to:

BBR Distribution, P.O. Box 625, Sheffield S1 3GY, United Kingdom
www.bbr-online.com/eahmh   distribution@bbr-online.com

EVENING LECTURE SERIES

Reaching Out to Mothers: Public Health and Child Welfare

Rima D. Apple

European Association for the History of Medicine and Health Publications
Sheffield 2002

European Association for the History of Medicine and Health
Officers and Members of the Scientific Board, 2001–2002

Reaching Out to Mothers: Public Health and Child Welfare
Rima D. Apple

First published in Great Britain in 2002
by European Association for the History of Medicine and Health Publications

Typeset by BBR Solutions Ltd, Chesterfield,
and printed in the UK by Peach Media Group, Chesterfield.

ISBN 0-9536522-6-2

European Association for the History of Medicine and Health Publications
Sheffield Centre for the History of Medicine
The University of Sheffield
Sheffield S10 2TN, UK

http://www.bbr-online.com/eahmh

Introduction

PROFESSOR RIMA D. APPLE is the first American scholar to lecture on the occasion of 'The Evening Lecture' in one of the regular Conferences of the European Association for the History of Medicine and Health. Her coming to Geneva – the place of the meeting being held on the theme of *Health and the Child: Culture and Care in History* – from the University of Wisconsin-Madison was both a gentle gift and an adventurous undertaking, since it took place only four days after the massacre of the Twin Towers and of the Pentagon and the subsequent troubles for air transportation from and to the United States of America. All attendants warmly acknowledged not only her exciting and beautifully argued paper, but also the testimony of her presence as a proof of real professional commitment.

Rima D. Apple is Professor of History within the Human Ecology and Women's Studies Programmes of the University of Wisconsin-Madison, affiliated to the Department of History of Medicine. Initially trained as a scientist (BA, Mathematics, 1961) she was lured by History of Science (MA, 1974) and then to History of Medicine (PhD, 1981). Her feminist activism (she belongs to the Women's Caucus of the History of Science Society) stands as a driving force in her career, and it has produced important results such as her associate editorship of the *Bibliographical Guide on the History of Women and Science* (1988, 1993) and her editorship of *Women, Health and Medicine in America, a Historical Handbook* (1990, 1992).

The publication in 1987 of *Mothers and Medicine. A Social History of Infant Feeding 1890–1950* made her known to the world audience and inaugurated two fruitful avenues of research. Focusing on the history of nutrition, her book *Vitamania: Vitamins in American Culture* (Rutgers University Press, 1996) has been honoured with the Kremers Award by the American Institute for the History of Pharmacy in 1998. However, the most relevant contributions by Professor Apple – or, at least, those which drove the organising committee to invite her to lecture at this particular event – lay on the side of the analysis of 'scientific motherhood'.

After her 1987 book, an outstanding article in *Social History of Medicine* (1995) – 'Constructing Mothers: Scientific Motherhood in the Nineteenth and Twentieth Centuries' – and the reader *Mothers and Motherhood. Readings in American History* (co-edited with Janet Golden, 1997), reflect the strength of the insight provided by feminist awareness on top of high standing scholarship, in the best tradition of the University of Wisconsin's History of Medicine Department. This lecture 'Reaching Out to Mothers: Public Health and Child Welfare' is but a further step forward on her serious exploration of the history of motherhood, a privileged construct to unravel the mixed landscape of biology, society and the professions. The paper, as such, focuses on the activities of the Wisconsin Bureau of Maternal and Child Health, mainly held in rural areas; which is a further interesting feature since most concerns have dealt so far with urban schemes.

Being connected so precisely to the main theme of the EAHMH Conference, this paper gives the flavour of a forthcoming new major work by the author. It was a great pleasure to have been among the first to be present at the display of the results of this ongoing research and it is a no less pleasant duty to make it possible to disseminate them.

Esteban Rodríguez-Ocaña
President, EAHMH

Notes on the Author

Rima D. Apple

RIMA D. APPLE is Professor at the University of Wisconsin-Madison, USA, in the School of Human Ecology and the Women's Studies Program, with an appointment in the Department of the History of Medicine. She has also held positions at the University of Melbourne, the University of Auckland, the University of Umea, the Norwegian University of Science and Technology (Trondheim) and the Wellcome Institute for the History of Medicine (London). She has published extensively on the women's health history, the history of motherhood, and the history of vitamin supplementation. Among her books are: *Mothers and Motherhood: Readings in American History* (Columbus, 1997), co-edited with Janet Golden, and *Vitamania: Vitamins in American Culture* (New Brunswick, 1996) which received the Kremers Award in 1998 from the American Institute of the History of Pharmacy. She is currently studying the relationship between mothers and health-care providers.

Reaching Out to Mothers:
Public Health and Child Welfare

Rima D. Apple

I N THE EARLY DECADES OF THE TWENTIETH CENTURY, high infant mortality
rates were a serious concern throughout the countries of the Western
world. Stretching around the globe from Australia and New Zealand in the
southern hemisphere to the United States, Canada and Europe in the
northern hemisphere, public health reformers campaigned to alleviate the
frightening death rates of mothers and young children, rates that adversely
affected the nation's image and jeopardized the nation's economic and
political bases.[1] In part these drives were fueled by the need for an expanding
labor force during a time of industrial expansion. The need for a growing
population was only a small part of the problem, though, because many
countries experienced an influx of immigrants that swelled their population.
Of greater concern was that these high mortality rates indicated a weakening
population base. What was required was a healthy population, which would
advertise the wellbeing of the nation. Each country felt the urgency to
respond the same issue – to lower the infant death rates and improve the
health of mothers and children. However, distinctive political, medical,
social and cultural conditions shaped their particular responses.

     In the United States, the political system and the structure of medical
practice significantly affected responses to this critical problem. Our political
system is based on a balance of powers, a balance between the powers of the
federal government and those of state governments, between those of state
governments and those of local communities. On many issues, in many areas,
it is not the federal government that controls the action, especially not in

the nineteenth and early twentieth centuries. Not surprisingly then, in this period, there was no strong, centralized health-care system in the US. Concerned reformers and health-care professionals created locally appropriate responses, often funded through philanthropy. In addition to this distinctive political structure, there was in the US a sharp line drawn between 'private medicine' (curative medicine, treatment for medical conditions) and 'public health' (preventive medicine often in form of health education). Physicians in private practice zealously guarded their arena, wary of any possible infringement by the public health movement that would undercut their position or their practice.

Before the First World War in the United States, then, medical and political constraints shaped the sporadic and generally local efforts developed to address the problems of maternal and child health. The settlement house movement most clearly exemplifies the contemporary philosophy of reform. In institutions such as Hull House in Chicago and the Henry Street Settlement House in New York City, visiting nurses and other concerned women established communities through which they could learn about and evaluate the problems and needs of local residents, often immigrants. Settlement houses encouraged socialization and education. For example, they developed recreational and instructional programs, such as sewing clubs at which mothers could prepare clothes for their children and exchange information. They brought nurses to the community to visit homes and provide health education.

Settlement houses were most commonly found in large cities with significant immigrant populations. Local organizations led reform efforts in smaller cities and towns across the United States. To take but one example: that of the Attic Angels Association of Madison, Wisconsin, created in 1889.[2] In that year, one of the town's debutantes learned that twins had been born into a poor family that had no money even to buy the most basic of infant clothing. She enlisted the help of some friends who joined in sewing clothes for the children. As their history relates. 'They also ransacked their attics for clothing for other ... members of the family.' (Evidently this is the origin of the name 'Attic Angels'. One of the fathers observed the young women loaded with clothes, coming down the stairs from an attic, and exclaimed that they looked like angels.) Soon the women took on other tasks to help their less fortunate sisters; they visited the homes of the poor, bathing new borns, nursing the sick; they made layettes and they held Christmas parties for poor children. In 1908, in order to provide more professional assistance, the Attic Angels sponsored the first visiting nurse service in Madison to bring modern, scientific infant-care advice to the city's residents.

Two other institutions developed in US cities during the late nineteenth century in an even more directed effort to ameliorate the high rate of infant mortality: Little Mothers' Clubs and milk stations. The experiences of Dr S. Josephine Baker (the director of New York City's Bureau of Child Hygiene, not the singer) prompted the establishment of the first Little Mothers' Clubs.

Baker's inspiration: 'a scrawny child of eight or nine, dirty and dishevelled, lugging a dirtier and more dishevelled baby which alternated between peevish wailing and sucking at something anonymous, crying all the louder when the little mother slapped it in understandable childish impatience with the nagging noise.' (Figure 1 illustrates the contemporary image of the 'little mother' problem.) This little mother, Baker believed, was 'innocently and ignorantly killing her thousands of children a year'. She could not be wished away. She was, unfortunately, inevitable given the economic need that sent her mother out to work, leaving her at home to care for her younger siblings. What these girls needed, what most girls needed because most girls would grow up to be mothers, was instruction in 'practical child-hygiene'. In 1910, with the help of supportive school principals and public health nurses, Baker established Little Mothers' Leagues throughout the city's public elementary schools. Their success exceeded her hopes as the girls not only absorbed instruction in scientific feeding and other aspects of infant care, they also became, in Baker's words, 'our most efficient missionaries' as they told mothers in the tenements all about their lessons, often through skits and plays.[3]

The work of the New York program convinced others to establish their own clubs and classes. The head of the Milwaukee's Bureau of Child Welfare, Dr E.T. Lobedan, introduced Little Mothers' Clubs into the state of Wisconsin. By 1913 the city had 15 classes with almost 2,000 girls enrolled. In 1911 and 1912 when the Babies' Dispensary in Cleveland demonstrated the importance of classes in infant care for young girls, the public school curriculum was expanded to include modern child-care courses.[4]

Milk stations, too, arose out of the recognition of a specific problem, in this case it was the connection between bottle feeding and poor infant health. Similar organizations were being established in France at the same time, but with significant differences. The French organizations were usually established and directed by physicians; in contrast, the name most commonly associated with US milk stations was Nathan Straus, a New York department store owner and philanthropist. Straus directed and financially supported the construction of several processing plants that distributed both pure pasteurized milk and six-ounce bottles of prepared milk formula through

Figure 1. 'Little Mother' (Source: *The child in the city: A handbook of the Child Welfare Exhibit at the Coliseum, May 11-May 25, 1911* (Chicago, IL, 1911)).

stations set up in various areas of the City. Within a decade, he had donated plants to Philadelphia and Chicago so that infants of those cities could also enjoy the benefits of pasteurized milk. The different motive forces behind the milk stations, medical practitioners in the French case and business-philanthropist in the US case, points to another significant contrast between the two models. At the French stations, the distribution of pure milk was one of many different activities designed to insure the health of the child; for example, typically physicians associated with the stations provided medical supervision and instructions to mothers on the hygienic care of their infants. In the US, however, milk stations were not generally medical institutions; basically they distributed milk and did little beyond that.

In the US, these efforts had some effect, at least locally. One study concluded that in the three years just prior to the opening of milk stations in New York over 6,000 infants died from diarrheal diseases; in the three years following the milk stations, the number had fallen to little over 5,200. Though heartened by such evidence, reformers were exasperated by how much still needed to be done. Lillian Wald, the nurse who established the Henry Street Settlement House, was particularly galled by the contrast between the vast attention paid by the US government to other matters such as the boll weevil, which was devastating the southern cotton crop, and the lack of attention paid to high rates of infant mortality. She and Florence Kelley, a Henry Street resident and president of the consumer and labor advocacy organization, the National Consumers' League, reduced their concern to a simple question: 'If the Government can have a department to take such an interest in the cotton crop [the US Department of Agriculture], why can't it have a bureau to look after the nation's child crop?' These formidable women presented their idea to President Theodore Roosevelt in 1903 and for many years after they consistently lobbied presidents and other national leaders. Finally, in 1912, the US Children's Bureau was established as a federal agency.[5]

The mandate of the Children's Bureau was clear and limited: 'to investigate and report ... upon all matters pertaining to the welfare of children and child life among all classes of our people.' Notice: the agency was to investigate and report, not treat. Yet, within its limited charge, the Bureau accomplished much in its first years. Under the direction of Julia Lathrop, a former resident of Hull House, it conducted well-publicized studies that highlighted connections between infant and maternal mortality and morbidity and poverty in rural and urban areas. It produced popular brochures for general distribution to mothers across the country, among them *Prenatal Care* in 1913, and *Infant Care* in 1914. The latter proved to be the most popular federal publication ever. Moreover, anxious mothers from all areas of the country, urban and rural, sent poignant letter after poignant letter to the Bureau requesting help. Compassionate staff members responded with advice and even money and, when appropriate, they requested local agencies assist mothers in need. These actions were well beyond the scope of the agency's legal authority and its meager resources; therefore, concerned staff members often drew from their own resources. While the Bureau staff strained at their legislatively mandated boundaries, reformers bridled at the limitations of an agency that could do little more than conduct studies and publish brochures.

Due to the constraints of the Children's Bureau legislation, reformers took a different tack, pushing for the enactment of a federal Maternity and Infancy Protection Act, the so-called Sheppard-Towner Act. Historians point to two primary reasons for passage of the Act in 1921. First, with the passage of the Constitutional Amendment for women's suffrage, politicians were interested in currying favor with the newly enfranchised voters. Second, in mobilizing for the First World War, the United States had examined thousands of men for military service. Medical reports concluded that approximately one-third of the men were unfit for military duty and, most importantly, that the defects leading to their rejection would not have occurred if they had received proper care during infancy. Though the bill passed, it was over the vehement opposition of the medical profession. Consequently, in order to appease physicians who believed that such legislation was the first step towards state medicine, the law was carefully crafted to differentiate between health education (which was publicly financed) and medical care (which was between the patient and the physician). In other words, Sheppard-Towner affirmed and reinforced the distinction between public health and private practice by providing matching grants to states to be used only for information and instruction in nutrition and hygiene, and for prenatal and child health clinics.

Child health clinics were not new with Sheppard-Towner, of course. Various local groups had conducted clinics since at least the early years of the twentieth century. African-American women's clubs had periodically set up clinics in the southern United States.[6] The Attic Angels in Madison, Wisconsin, had established its first baby clinic in the summer of 1915; there infants and pre-school children could be weighed and measured and mothers could be advised on diet, care and training of their children.

A similar innovation developed primarily in agricultural regions of the United States, the better baby contests (Figure 2). These usually consisted of an individual consultation with the mother and instruction both

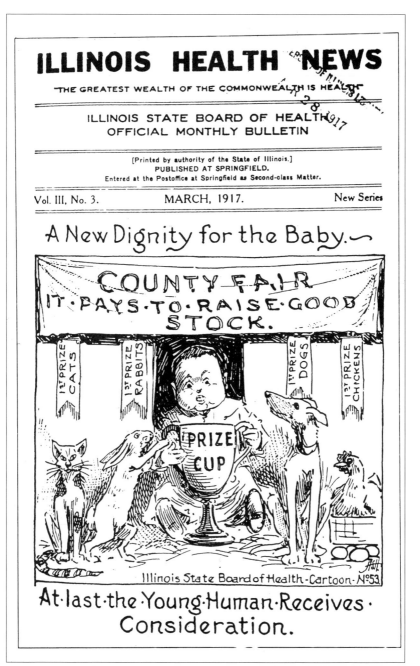

Figure 2. Better Baby Content (Source: *Illinois Health News*, March 1917).

Figure 3. Wisconsin Child Health Special trailer (Source: Wisconsin Historical Society, Visual Archives, Series 2253, Maternal and Child Health).

in the form of printed material that the mother could take home to study and in public lectures and exhibits on contemporary child-care advice. Each child was rated and those with the highest ratings were declared the winners. The contests satisfied two important public health goals. First, they could identify potential health problems and direct mothers to physicians for treatment. Second, since health reformers anticipated that winners would be prime examples of modern infant care, the winning mothers would act as role models and their babies would provide living examples of the importance of scientific child care.[7] Of course, the results did not always reflect expectations. An article with the headline 'Best babies are blow to science', gleefully announced that the winners named at the conclusion of one such 1916 contest confounded the experts. All three gold medals went to children of 'working men', whose wives unambiguously claimed that they did not use or need 'new fangled ideas'. The mother of George Carlin, winner in the 18 months to two year category, told reporters, 'I raised this baby to suit myself. I didn't listen to any faddish rules or read any books on how to raise a baby. I raised him myself and I guess I haven't made a failure of it.' The mothers of the other winners similarly eschewed modern theories.

Though clinics did not originate with the Sheppard-Towner Act, nonetheless the funding that accompanied the legislation did significantly encourage the spread of clinics into new areas, for example state funding of clinics in rural areas. The state of Wisconsin initially used the federal monies to outfit the Wisconsin Child Health Special, a moveable venue for health clinics (Figure 3). Staffed by nurses and physicians from the state's Bureau of Maternal and Child Health, this trailer travelled from village to town to crossroads offering clinics in rural areas. The work of the Special was augmented with clinics sponsored by local and philanthropic organizations and staffed by Bureau personnel. Figure 4 demonstrates some of the materials available to mothers who attended Wisconsin's rural child-health clinics. (The mother is shielding her face with a copy of *Child Management*, one of the many pamphlets produced by the US Children's Bureau.) Other activities included expanded educational programs. For example, some states distributed copies of the federal *Prenatal Care* and *Infant Care* to new mothers. Many other states used Sheppard-Towner funds to create their own versions of these pamphlets, which they sent to mothers throughout the state to instruct them on scientific infant care.

The focus on child health clinics and publications is indicative of the philosophy of reform that predominated in the years following the First World War in the United States. Though educational efforts such as these were not unique to this period, the emphasis on them represents a narrowing

Figure 4. Rural child health clinic, Wisconsin, c.1935 (Source: Wisconsin Historical Society, Visual Archives, Series 2253, Maternal and Child Health).

of focus from community to individual. Earlier efforts such as settlement houses, Attic Angels and milk stations placed the problem of maternal and infant health into a larger social and even cultural context, recognizing the interrelationship between poverty and other environmental factors and poor health, and found only part of the solution in maternal education. However, by the second decade of the twentieth century, reformers more and more emphasized the deleterious affects of maternal ignorance and the absolute need for education, though few would have gone so far as one mother, writing in the popular women's magazine *Good Housekeeping* in 1911. This self-styled modern 'trained mother' acknowledged the importance of 'maternal instinct', which she described as 'love, patience, and unselfishness', but she went further to claim that 'maternal instinct left alone succeeds in killing a large proportion of the babies born into this world'.[8] Health-care professionals too stressed the primacy of maternal education, reporting that 'Those babies whose mothers were able and willing to exercise intelligent supervision did well in spite of the most unfavorable conditions, while those who were deprived of intelligent care did badly no matter how favorable the other factors might be.'[9] Public health efforts of the period reflected these observations with activities that privileged maternal education, including instruction on the importance of medical supervision, over more environmental or systemic solutions to the problem of infant and maternal mortality and morbidity.

Sheppard-Towner was successful in expanding public health efforts in the areas of maternal and child health. However, despite its attempts to rigorously differentiate 'public health' and 'private medicine', opposition from the medical profession to the legislation continued unabated. At the same time, politicians came to recognize that such legislation was not particularly useful in attracting the woman voter. Consequently, the support that had made its passage possible evaporated and Sheppard-Towner was not renewed; it expired in 1929. Local and private efforts, such as Attic Angels and the work of African-American women's clubs, continued but on a smaller scale than that possible with federal support.

Then, in 1935, in the depths of the Depression, federal funding once again became available. The Social Security Act included funding for maternal and child health in rural areas. And once again, the monies were intended for education, not treatment. The funding made it possible for the state's nurses to expand the scope of the activities of the Bureau of Maternal and Child Health. In addition to their educational programs and their well-child clinics, they added an important new dimension to their work: home visits. These visits brought them into closer contact with their clients.

Rather than seeing mothers only intermittently at temporary health clinics, now the nurses established a more regularized routine, identifying potential clients and scheduling repeat visits. Acutely aware of their role as public health workers, they were careful to maintain a positive relationship with the local physicians and to direct appropriate cases to them. They were always mindful that theirs was an educational, advisory role, subsidiary to that of the physician.

The public health nurses were assigned counties throughout the rural areas of Wisconsin. Within her county, the nurse began by locating pregnant women, new mothers and pre-school children. Unlike the urban public health nurse who could canvass by blocks, the nurses in rural Wisconsin covered vast areas, travelling by car and even by foot. Catherine McLetchie graphically described her attempt to call on a family living deep in the woods:

> It was necessary to leave the car with neighbors, and walk through several fields, in one of which a bull was tethered. He seemed only mildly interested in the nurse, who luckily was wearing blue, not red! After walking through woods, up and down hills, and crawling under two fences, in twenty minutes or so the house was reached. Then the whole process was repeated on the return journey. It was a very hot, tired and perspiring nurse that finally reached the car and relaxed somewhat behind the wheel.[10]

If another nurse had resided in the county earlier, her records could provide a starting point for locating clients. Elizabeth Murrisy in Marathon County was gratified that her predecessor 'had built up the prenatal case load. Wherever I went,' she noted in her reports back to the Bureau's office, 'it seemed noticeable that maternal work is so much easier to do.' Nurses also had lists of women who had attended previous Bureau clinics. In addition, some local physicians referred their patients to Bureau nurses for instruction in appropriate infant care. When a nurse first arrived in the county, she would visit each of the physicians there to discuss the Bureau's work and the Standing Orders that shaped her work. The physicians had the option of agreeing with the Standing Orders or making modifications for their patients. Lectures that the nurses often gave to local women's and girls' organizations and in the local high schools proved fruitful sources for information about potential new clients. So too did neighbors and relatives. Hazel Nordley, who worked in northern Wisconsin in 1940, found that neighbors were crucial. Moreover, Nordley recognized that the early days following birth are critical 'teaching moments', or, as she explained, 'The mothers have so many questions to ask about the new babies and it always seems as if there is so much information to be given at this time.' Therefore, she devised a unique system for reaching new mothers promptly: she gave each pregnant woman she saw a mimeographed postcard, asking her to complete and mail the card immediately after birthing. Mothers evidently appreciated her consideration and within months of beginning the program, Nordley reported that many of the cards were being returned quickly.

Nurses found that one of the most popular forums for dispensing advice was the demonstration bath. Nordley determined that among young mothers especially 'this service is appreciated a great deal' and that even 'mothers who have children have asked for the bath demonstration'. Ruth Exner in Grant County made a special effort to speak to mothers early in the postpartum period because she realized that, in her words, 'young mothers are anxious to learn simpler ways of taking care of their new babies. One thing in particular is the baby's bath tray which has appealed to so many.' In other instances, nurses used the demonstration bath to help a new mother become more comfortable with her infant. Lelia Johnson described one such instance in her report from western Wisconsin: 'Demonstration baby bath was given to Mrs H***, as this mother lost a baby two years ago with naval [sic] infection and now is afraid to handle and bath the baby.' Many nurses apparently used the demonstration of a bath as an opening wedge to initiate discussion of other aspects of child care. Thelma Burke understood that a mother could use this practical instruction to learn more. 'I've given one infant demonstration bath where the mother "fired" questions at me,' she reported from north-central Wisconsin. Though this young mother was eager to hear about modern concepts, Burke despaired of her practicing them because, 'Since Grandma, who came from Poland, lives there too, it might be very difficult for the mother to do what she really wants.'

In the late 1930s, the bureau produced a 16mm, silent film that depicted the many intricate steps involved in modern, medically sanctioned infant bathing, which was shown in infant-care classes at temporary Health Centers, in high schools and among community groups (Figure 5). It opens with the mother scrubbing her hands and arms up to the elbows, then she washes the infant's eyes and ears with dampened sterile cotton, weighs the baby, washes the infant's face with a wash cloth, soaps the baby on a changing table, places the baby in a basin and rinses her, dries the baby and then oils her, before dressing her in a light shirt and diaper.[11] Given the demands of this 'appropriate infant bath', involving sterile cotton, separate washcloth and basin, special 'mild baby soap' and the like, it is doubtful that many of the poor, exhausted mothers could continue similar routines daily without the assistance of the County Demonstration Nurse. Whether poverty-stricken mothers could or would follow through on the nurse's

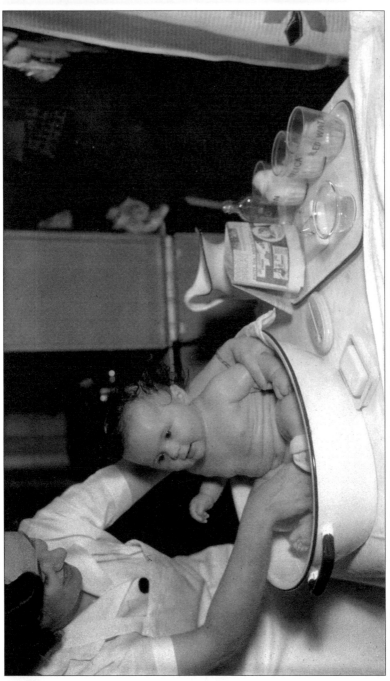

Figure 5. Bathing the baby, from the film *From morning to night*, c.1937 (Source: Wisconsin Historical Society, Visual Archives).

instructions, or merely wanted another pair of hands helping the family, mothers' interests in infant bathing nonetheless indicates their appreciation of the assistance health-care experts could provide them.

Even in the Depression, not all residents of rural Wisconsin were economically hard-pressed. Nurses would sometimes write about better-off and better-educated mothers. But more often, their reports were filled with sad stories of lack of resources, lack of knowledge, lack of emotion and energy. In August 1936, one nurse visited Mrs J** L** G*** who, she reported, 'Lives a million miles from nowhere and is about ready to deliver. Has no plans for delivery and absolutely nothing to work with.' In this case the nurse had an alternative to a poorly equipped home birth. The husband was of Native American parentage. Consequently, his wife was entitled to use a hospital in northern Wisconsin that had been especially established for Native Americans, a trip the nurse quickly arranged with the local relief department.

Nurses encountered clients who either would not or could not cope with the advice given them. Most commonly mothers' inability to act on a nurse's instructions resulted from economic and social conditions beyond their control. Wisconsin farmers were hard hit during the Depression and families mobilized the labor of all able-bodied, and perhaps less than able-bodied members. In September 1937, a nurse movingly described one family she frequently visited:

> Called at the J*** S*** house; guess conditions will never improve. Mrs S***
> was out in the hay field and baby being cared for by 12-year-old girl. House
> filthy. Did not give her advice re: the poor puny baby as she looked too worn
> out to care what happened.

In the homes of Native Americans, Polish and Irish immigrants, and native-born residents, nurses would discover that pregnant women close to their delivery date did not have the most essential items of a layette or supplies necessary for home birthing. Often these dilapidated houses were without basic utilities such as running water. One nurse very clearly recognized the problem; she explained:

> Cannot pay M.D. any more than $15.00 and that is on time. Relief pays only
> $15.00 for delivery. M.D. can'st [sic] have anywhere from 8 to 16 prenatal visits,
> delivery, driving anywhere from 5 to 40 miles, postnatal visits, and postnatal
> examinations for $15.00 a case and not lost [sic] money. These mothers can't
> have proper food, cod liver oil, and calcium.

In many cases lack of financial resources made it difficult, if not impossible, for rural mothers to follow the advice of public health nurses who visited them, much less travel to see physicians and follow their advice.

Still the nurses persisted in their rounds, instructing mothers in modern infant-care and directing them to physicians for prenatal and postpartum care. Nurses wrote gleefully of clients who dutifully followed medical advice, yet just as often they expressed frustration over what they perceived was their clients' lack of appreciation for modern scientific infant care. They would discover that mothers would listen attentively to their advice and promise to observe it; however, on return visits it was clear that little had changed. Nurse Alice Rude faced just such a situation. She wondered if more frequent visits would ameliorate conditions. Did her clients 'need a little more supervision at proper intervals,' she queried rhetorically in her report from central Wisconsin, or is it 'wasting time to visit them'? Nordley believed that the 'threat' of more intense supervision could persuade clients to visit the doctor early in their pregnancies. Not all her clients were eager to do so, but they went. As Nordley concluded, 'Some of them are a little reluctant about going but perhaps they will feel they would rather go than to tell me they haven't been there when I call again.'

The nurses were strong in their belief of the efficacy of modern infant care, but their somewhat restricted mandate placed them in a conundrum. On the one hand, nurses had to teach their clients of the significance and efficacy of medically supervised maternal and child care, clients whom we have seen were not necessarily able or willing to follow their directions. On the other hand, there were times when the nurses' recommendations conflicted with those of local physicians. Aware of the importance of a positive relationship with those physicians, nurses found ways to convey their ideas to mothers without apparently contradicting physicians. For example, Rude worried because physicians in her county in central Wisconsin did not advise mothers to boil the milk they fed their babies. Her solution: in her words, she 'diplomatically told' the women to 'scald the milk in a double boiler for a few minutes.'

These County Demonstration Nurses were on the front lines, so to speak, of the reform efforts to curb high rates of infant mortality and improve infant and maternal health. From their narrative reports sent regularly back to the Bureau, we learn about the difficulties they had walking the line that separated 'public health' and 'private medicine'. They had very clear ideas about appropriate modern child care: it was based on the most up-to-date science and it required directing their clients to medical practitioners for prenatal care and labor and delivery, as well as postpartum and infant care; it reflected generally accepted middle-class standards of the period.[12] Their focus, like that of other public health workers and reformers in these years, was on maternal responsibility and improving child health through the education of the mother. Yet we sense in their writings something almost akin to 'culture shock', as these nurses faced people with resources too limited to act on modern, medical precepts of infant care. In the work of the County Demonstration nurses of Wisconsin we also recognize the obstacles created by rural poverty and the gulf between idealized urban practices and rural reality.

As these studies of public health reforms document, there is no simple, one-size-fits-all answer to the dilemma of high rates of infant mortality. The tension between federal and state control, the concern to preserve a distinct line between public health and private medicine limited the effectiveness of the programs developed in the United States in the early twentieth century. Moreover, ignoring the financial conditions and geographical circumstances of mothers and children, while emphasizing maternal education and mothers' responsibilities, engendered programs that could not address the root causes of the problem. In particular, the narrative reports of the Wisconsin nurses remind us that meaningful solutions must focus not only on narrowly defined medical indicators, but must also evaluate each situation within its social, cultural, political and environmental milieu. These nurses recognized these difficulties and strove to bring the best of contemporary infant care to their clients, within the constraints of local and national politics and of the US medical system. As such their stories stand both as a cautionary tale of the limits of particularized responses and a symbol of possibility.

Notes

1   There have been a growing number of studies of these questions in the past several decades. For information on developments outside the United States, this essay draws heavily on a wide variety of histories of maternal and child health that has emerged, especially in the past two decades. Among the most useful for this study are: Jane Lewis, *The politics of motherhood: Child and maternal welfare in England, 1900–1939* (London, 1980); Lara Marks, *Model mothers: Jewish mothers and maternity provision in East London, 1870–1939* (New York, 1994); Linda Bryder, *Not just weighing babies: Plunket in Auckland, 1908–1998* (Auckland, 1998); Philippa Mein Smith, *Mothers and king baby: Infant survival and welfare in an imperial world: Australia, 1880–1950* (Houndville, 1997); Alisa Klaus, *Every child a lion: The origins of infant and maternal health policy in the United States and France, 1890–1920* (Ithaca, 1993); Anne La Berge, 'Mothers and infants, nurses and nursing: Alfred Donne and the medicalization of child care in nineteenth-century France', *Journal of the History of Medicine*, 46 (1991), 20–43.

For the situation in the United States, see especially, Rima D. Apple, *Mothers and medicine: A social history of infant feeding, 1890–1950* (Madison, 1987); Molly Ladd-Taylor, *Mother-work: Women, child welfare, and the state, 1890–1930* (Urbana, 1994); Kriste Lindemeyer, '*A right to childhood*': *US Children's Bureau and child welfare, 1912–1946* (Urbana, 1997); Richard Meckel, '*Save the babies*': *American public health reform and the prevention of infant mortality, 1850–1929* (Baltimore, 1990).

There have been some recent studies looking particularly at rural conditions, for example, Julia Grant, 'Caught between common sense and science: The Cornell Child Study Clubs, 1925–1945', *History of Education Quarterly*, 34 (1994), 433–52; Lynn Curry, *Modern mothers in the heartland: Gender, health, and progress in Illinois, 1900–1930* (Columbus, 1999); Sean Patrick Adams, '"Who guards our mothers, who champions our kids?" Amy Louise Hunter and maternal and child health in Wisconsin, 1935–1960', *Wisconsin Magazine of History*, 83 (2000), 181–201. Older but still useful sources include Frances Sage Bradley and Margaretta A. Williamson, *Rural children in selected counties of North Carolina* (Washington, DC, 1918); Viola I. Paradise, *Maternity care and the welfare of young children in a homesteading county of Montana* (Washington, DC, 1919); Florence Brown Sherbon and Elizabeth Moore, *Maternity and infant care in two rural counties in Wisconsin* (Washington, DC, 1919); Mary Breckinridge, *Wide neighborhoods: A history of the Frontier Nursing Service* (New York, 1952). But much work still needs to be done on the history of rural maternal and child health reform efforts. This close investigation of the day-to-day work of the nurses of the Bureau of Maternal and Child Health of Wisconsin's Department of Health suggests potentially insightful areas of new and comparative research among states in the US and across national boundaries. For a suggestive beginning, see Linda Bryder, 'Two models of infant welfare in the first half of the twentieth century: New Zealand and the United States' and Rima D. Apple, 'Educating mothers: The Wisconsin Bureau of Maternal and Child Health', presented at 'Women's bodies, women's history: Conversations across time & culture', an international, interdisciplinary conference held at the University of Melbourne, June 2001.

2   Information on Attic Angels is drawn from Attic Angel Association Papers, Madison, Wisconsin, 1898–1960, in the Wisconsin Historical Society, Microforms Department, reels P94-1972, P94-1973, P94-1974.

3   For more on Baker's work in her own words, see S. Josephine Baker, *Fighting for life* (New York, 1939, reprint edition 1980), esp. pp. 131–37.

4   For more on these, see Apple, *Mothers and medicine*, esp. pp. 102–03, 127.

5   The information on the Children's Bureau has been drawn from Molly Ladd-Taylor, *Raising a baby the government way: Mothers' letters to the Children's Bureau, 1915–1932* (New Brunswick, 1986; Lindemeyer, 'A right to child hood'; Emily K. Abel, 'Correspondence between Julia C. Lathrop, Chief of the Children's Bureau, and a working-class woman, 1914–1915', *Journal of Women's History*, 5 (1993), 79–88; Nancy Pottisham Weiss, 'The mother-child dyad revisited: Perceptions of mothers and children in twentieth-century child-rearing manuals', *Journal of Social Issues*, 34 (1978), 29–45.

6   Susan L. Smith, *Sick and tired of being sick and tired: Black women's health activism in America, 1890–1950* (Philadelphia, 1995).

7   For more on better baby contests, see Annette K. Vance Dorsey, *Better baby contests: The scientific quest for perfect childhood health in the early twentieth century* (Jefferson, NC, 1999).

8   'A trained mother', 'Maternal instinct run riot', *Good Housekeeping*, 52 (1911), 245–47.

9   Richard M. Smith, 'The important causes of infant mortality', *Child Health Bulletin*, 5 (1929), 97–109. Quotation on p. 103.

10 All material from the County Demonstration Nurses is drawn from the nurses' reports which can be found in Wisconsin Bureau of Maternal & Child Health, Series 2253, Boxes 10–13, 'Wisconsin. Bureau of Maternal & Child Health. Programs & Demonstrations, 1922-61', held at the Wisconsin Historical Society, Madison, WI.

11 'From morning until night' (c.1937) is located in the Iconographic Archives of the Wisconsin Historical Society.

12 Rima D. Apple, 'Constructing mothers: Scientific motherhood in the nineteenth and twentieth centuries', *Social History of Medicine*, 8 (1995), 161–78.

EAHMH Publications Evening Lecture Series

The main feature of EAHMH's bi-annual meetings is to create a stimulating atmosphere which enables an intensive yet informal exchange of ideas between young researchers and well established scholars. In that context it has become a tradition to invite a distinguished academic to present part of his or her own work, at their discretion, so that the essence of a long-standing professional pre-occupation with medical history might emerge in individual and exemplary ways.

Current titles in the series are:

Reaching Out to Mothers: Public Health and Child Welfare
by Rima D. Apple (2002: ISBN 0-9536522-6-2)

Harvey's Troubles with the Egg
by Esther Fischer-Homberger (2001: ISBN 0-9536522-3-8)

The Human Body, from Slavery to the Biomarket: An Ethical Analysis
by Giovanni Berlinguer (1999: ISBN 0-9536522-1-1)

Improving Health: A Challenge to European Medieval Galenism
by Luis García-Ballester (1996: ISBN 0-9527045-3-6)

Ethics in Medicine: Historical Aspects of the Present Debate
by Eduard Seidler (1996: ISBN 0-9527045-2-8)

See our website at www.bbr-online.com/eahmh for detailed descriptions of all these titles, plus current titles in the EAHMH History of Medicine, Health and Disease Series, Network Series, and Research Guide Series.